7/92
6

PA TWFCF99

D0579842

3

PAT

WHERE FOOD COMES FROM

DOROTHY HINSHAW PATENT

photographs by William Muñoz

Holiday House / New York

Text copyright © 1991 by Dorothy Hinshaw Patent
Photographs copyright © 1991 by William Muñoz
All rights reserved
Printed in the United States of America
First Edition

Library of Congress Cataloging-in-Publication Data

Patent, Dorothy Hinshaw.
Where food comes from / by Dorothy Hinshaw Patent ;
photographs by William Muñoz.—1st ed.
p.   cm.
Includes index.
Summary: Shows how all food—grains, vegetables, fruits,
and dairy and meat products—begins on the farm
as sun, earth, air, and water combine to grow plants.
ISBN 0-8234-0877-9
1. Food—Juvenile literature.   2. Food crops—Juvenile literature.
3. Animal food—Juvenile literature.   [1. Food.]   I. Muñoz,
William, ill. II. Title.
TX355.P26   1991
641.3—dc20
90-49833   CIP   AC
ISBN 0-8234-0877-9

Contents

CHAPTER ONE

Food Starts with the Sun

When you go to the grocery store or sit down to dinner, do you ever wonder where your food comes from? Your family buys food in boxes and bottles, cans and jars. Meat comes neatly cut and wrapped in plastic. But how did all that food start out? Where, after all, does food really come from?

Trucks carry fresh fruits and vegetables from the farms where they are grown. They may then travel by train, plane, or truck to where they will be sold. Animals raised for meat are brought by truck or train to slaughterhouses, where they are killed. The meat is then sent to the stores. More and more food, however, is processed before your family buys it. That means that different ingredients are all taken to a factory where the food is made. Cake mixes, taco shells, frozen dinners, crackers, cookies, and many other foods are made in factories, where they are packaged before being sent to the store.

But even the most ready-made food, like a frozen TV dinner, begins at the same place—the farm. And at the farm, all food starts out from the same sources—the sun, the earth, and the air.

Plants do the most important work in making food. Leaves contain a green substance called chlorophyll. The chlorophyll traps energy from the sun. The plant uses the energy to produce sugar that in turn helps it grow.

A pea plant grows straight up toward the sky.

Starting out as a tiny green sprout, the plant grows stems and leaves, flowers and fruit. As the stems grow above the ground, the roots branch out underground, anchoring the plant firmly.

The roots of plants are important in making food. They take water and minerals from the soil. The roots of many plants, like peas and beans, can also take nitrogen from air pockets in the soil.

The water is combined with carbon dioxide from the air to make the sugars. Minerals are added to make other chemicals the plant needs to grow. Once a plant has grown, it can become food.

This parsley plant has plenty of roots to absorb water and minerals from the soil.

Animals like cows get all their nourishment from eating plants.

We get our food in two ways. We can eat the plants themselves. Or we can eat the animals that feed on the plants. All our food comes either from plants or the animals that eat them.

Food gives us many different nutrients, or things we must eat to be healthy. Protein is important for all living things. It is the main material for building bodies, especially muscles. Foods like chicken, dried beans, nuts, lean meats, fish, milk, and eggs contain lots of protein.

Carbohydrates are sugars and starches. We can eat sugar in honey, cookies, fruits, and other sweet foods. Starches are found in pasta, cereal, bread, and tortillas. Carbohydrates are especially important in giving our body energy.

Foods like butter and salad oil are made of fats. We need small amounts of fat to help build our nervous systems and other body parts. But mostly, fats give us concentrated energy.

Food contains additional important nutrients, too. Fruits and vegetables have fiber, which we need for good digestion. They also have vitamins and minerals that help our bodies work well. Besides giving us protein, meat provides us with the mineral iron and some vitamins.

By eating lots of different foods, we give our body the nutrients it needs to grow and be healthy.

These vegetable products contain important nutrients like fats, carbohydrates, protein, vitamins, and minerals.

CHAPTER TWO

Vegetables and Fruits

Fruits and vegetables are our most colorful foods, from bright green peas to orange carrots and shiny red apples. We eat every part of a plant in one food or another.

When we eat lettuce and spinach, we are using leaves for food, whereas celery stalks are really leaf stems. The stems of sugarcane are harvested for the sweet sugar they contain.

A stalk of celery.

This is how Red Delicious apples look on a tree.

Lettuce comes in many shapes and can be red as well as green.

Carrots grow in the ground.

A fat red radish straight from the garden.

Carrots and radishes are roots. Plants like these don't flower their first year. Instead, they produce lots of leaves and then store energy in a thick root. If a radish or carrot is not picked, the following spring it will send up a flower stalk, using the energy stored in the root to produce flowers and seeds.

The white strand to the right of the center is one of the underground stems that grow potatoes.

Potatoes grow underground like roots, but they are actually special stems, called tubers. The potato plant stores energy in the tubers, which wait underground through the winter. In the springtime, stems grow from the tubers, making new potato plants.

Onion bulbs look like roots, too, but they aren't. If you cut an onion in half from top to bottom, you will see that it is made up of thickened leaves growing from the base of the bulb. These leaves store energy for the onion plant during the winter.

When the onions are ready for harvest, the bulbs are pulled from the ground and dried. Then the tops are cut off before the onions are taken to the store.

The clusters of flowers that make up the head of a cauliflower grow at the top of the plant's stem, surrounded by leaves.

Have you ever imagined eating flowers? Well, you do eat them if you dine on broccoli or cauliflower. A head of either of these vegetables is actually a huge cluster of thousands of tiny unopened flowers. If broccoli is left on the plant instead of being picked, it produces many small yellow flowers.

After flowers bloom, they are pollinated. This means the male pollen is carried to the female egg cells. The pollen gets there in different ways. Insects like bees pollinate flowers when they hunt for nectar. Some flowers are pollinated by the wind. Once the flowers are pollinated, seeds are made. Many plants produce special seed protectors. When we eat green string beans, we are enjoying the pod of the bean plant, which holds the seeds inside. If the bean pod is left on the plant, it will swell up with seeds and then dry out. The dried pod splits open, releasing seeds that can grow into new plants. The beans used in chili and navy bean soup are the dried seeds of bean plants.

Some plants use fruits to help spread their seeds. Fruits are tasty to animals as well as to us. When an animal eats a fruit, it swallows the seeds, too. The seeds aren't digested. When they come out in the animal's droppings, they are "planted" in a new place.

The green bean pod (*center*) is ready to pick.

A bell pepper ready for picking.

Some vegetables, like peppers, are really fruits. If we open up a pepper, we can see tiny seeds clinging to the inside. Tomatoes are also fruits.

Tomato fruits start out green, then gradually change to a ripe red.

Strawberries grow on small plants close to the ground.

We eat many fruits that hold the seeds in different ways. Each little round bit of raspberry contains one seed. Blueberries have several small seeds inside, while the tiny strawberry seeds are on the outside of the fruit.

So far, no one has devised a seedless apple, but some kinds of oranges lack seeds.

Large fruits, like apples and oranges, grow on trees. The seeds of the apple are in the core, while orange seeds are near the center.

Some fruits are seedless. These are not natural. They have been developed by people to make eating them easier. Such fruits must be grown in special ways to get new plants.

We also eat the ripe seeds of plants, like nuts. They are very rich in nutrients, especially fats and protein. Much of the seed is stored energy that the new plant uses until it's big enough to make its own food. Seeds contain so much fat that some kinds are used to make oil for cooking and for salad dressings. Sunflower seeds, safflower seeds, and soybeans are often pressed for their oil.

Sunflowers are grown for the seeds that form in the large center of the flower.

This is how the peas look inside the pod.

Peas are the seeds of the pea plant. Like beans, peas grow in pods. Chinese snow peas are a kind of pea pod picked while the seeds are still tiny. Snap peas are a special kind of pea with a juicy, tender pod. Both the snap pea pod and the peas inside are good to eat.

CHAPTER THREE

The Grains

The seeds of some grasses, called grains, are the most important kind of food in the world. Grasses are different from most other plants we eat, since they are simpler, with no real stems. Their flowers are pollinated by the wind rather than by bees.

Grains provide more nutrition to people than all other foods. Wheat, rice, rye, oats, and corn are all grains. Grains are also fed to animals, such as cattle and lambs.

Grains are rich in nutrients, like fats and protein. One grain—corn—is pressed for its oil.

Grains, especially wheat and corn, are the main ingredient in many of our foods.

Here are three major grains (*left to right*)—rice, oats, and wheat.

Close-up of the dry, dented kernels of field corn.

Corn is used in many other ways, too. Sweet corn is a wonderful summertime treat eaten fresh from the cob. Frozen and canned corn are sweet corn that has been removed from the cobs and stored so that it can be eaten later.

Most of the corn farmers grow, however, is not sweet corn. It is called field corn and has a wonderful flavor all of its own. Field corn is dried and ground to make cornmeal, which is used for muffins, corn bread, and tortillas. Field corn is also fed to animals to fatten them up.

We eat rice whole. The dried grains are cooked in water to moisten and soften them. When the outer covering is left on the grains, we call it brown rice. White rice is made by polishing the grains to remove the brown husk.

Oatmeal is made by drying the grains of oats and flattening them with special machines. Oat bran, which contains healthy fiber, is the outer covering of the oat seeds.

Wheat is the most commonly used of all grains. Most wheat is ground into flour. Whole wheat flour is made by grinding the whole grain. To make white flour, the bran and the wheat germ (the part of the grain that would grow into a new plant) are removed. Flour is used for making breads, cakes, cookies, and pie crust. Rye is another grain used mostly as flour.

Wheat is grown in vast fields that stretch to the horizon.

CHAPTER FOUR

Meat

When we eat meat, we are actually eating the cooked muscles of animals. We raise a variety of animals for meat. In the United States, cattle are the most important. Beef, including hamburger and steaks, comes from cattle. The meat from young cattle (or calves) is also eaten. It is called veal.

Some meat products from the supermarket.

This beef cow might be kept for breeding or slaughtered for meat.

Cuts of beef from different parts of the animal. The chuck (*left*), comes from the shoulder. Rib steak (*next*) is from the chest area. T-bone steak comes from the middle of the back. The T-shaped bone is part of the animal's backbone. Round steak (*right*) comes from the top of the hind leg.

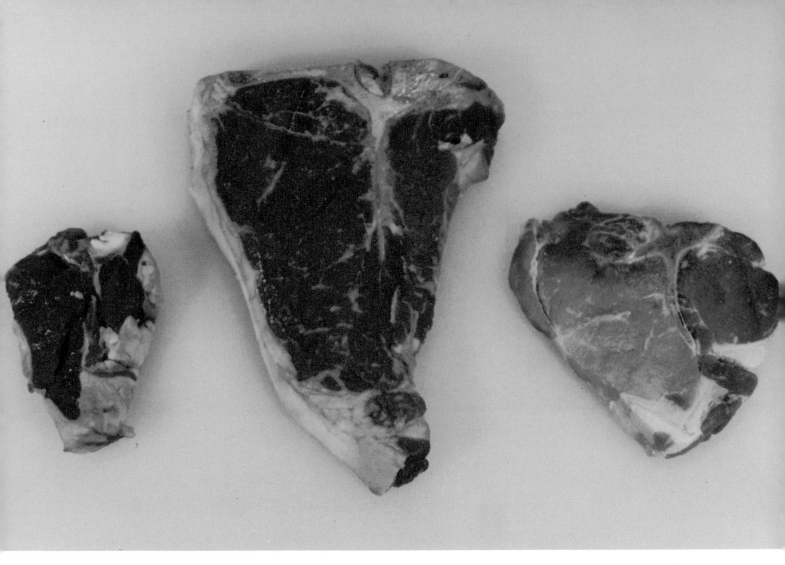

The lamb chop (*left*) and pork chop (*right*) come from the same part of the animal as the T-bone steak (*center*).

Pork, too, is an important meat for us. Pork comes from pigs and is usually not eaten fresh. It is preserved, or cured. For example, ham is a large muscle from the hind leg of the pig that is treated with salt and other chemicals to preserve it and give it a pink color. Some hams are also hung over a slow-burning fire to give them a smoky flavor.

Pigs grow fast and are slaughtered before they are full grown.

Like ham, bacon is cured pork. It comes from the belly of the pig. The streaks of pink in the bacon are muscle and the white part is fat. Bacon is also sometimes smoked.

In some parts of the world, sheep are the most common meat animals. The meat from adult sheep is called mutton, while lamb comes from young sheep.

Cows, pigs, and sheep are all mammals—animals with fur that feed their young on milk. Besides eating meat from mammals, we eat birds like chickens and turkeys, called poultry.

A flock of domesticated turkeys.

We enjoy many other products made from meat, too. Sausages like bologna, pepperoni, salami, and hot dogs can be made from beef, pork, poultry, or a mixture of them. Spices are added to sausages for flavor.

Fish is becoming a popular food in America today. Once canned tuna was the only fish many people ate. Now fresh fish from around the world can be found in supermarkets.

Sometimes the origin of food is surprising. Gelatin, used to make dessert products like Jell-O, is an animal product. It comes from the connective tissues that bind one bone to another and attach muscles to bones.

The seafood shown here comes from around the world, including Alaskan king salmon (*right*) and Australian lobster tails (*below, middle*).

CHAPTER FIVE

Riches from Hens and Cows

We get dairy products from animals without killing them. For example, chicken eggs are considered dairy products. The female chickens, called hens, lay the eggs. Unlike wild female birds that mate, lay eggs, and sit on them until they hatch, hens can lay eggs without mating. Even if the eggs were kept warm, they would never hatch into chicks.

Milk is used to make many different foods. It is also added to bread, cakes, cookies, and pudding.

A brown Swiss cow. The ear tags identify her.

We often eat eggs for breakfast, but they are important in other foods, too. Custards are made mostly from eggs and so are soufflés. Eggs are also used in cakes, some ice cream, and breads, cookies, and many other foods.

In America, almost all the milk we drink comes from cows. But in some other countries, people drink milk from animals like goats, sheep, and horses.

Female mammals produce milk to feed their young. The milk is made and stored in a sac called an udder under the animal's body. The young mammal sucks on the fingerlike teats of the udder to get the milk.

After a dairy cow gives birth, the calf is usually taken away and fed separately. Then the cow is milked by hand or by a milking machine. The milker pulls on the teat as a calf would with its mouth, and the milk squirts out.

Milk comes from the teats on the cow's udder.

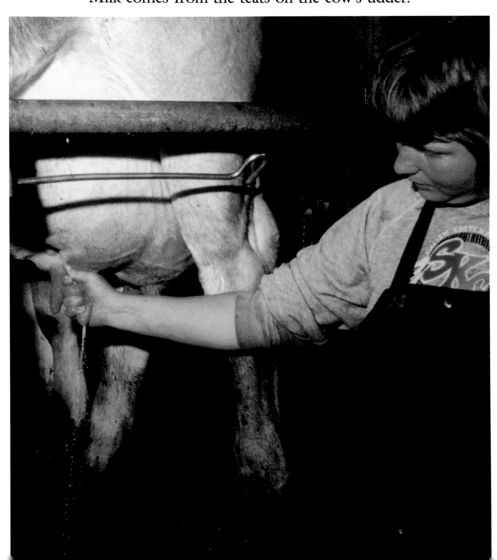

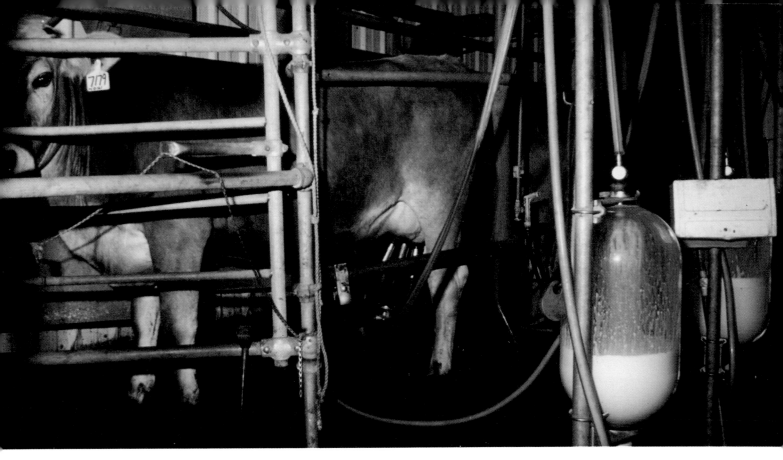

This cow is being milked by machine. You can see the fresh, creamy milk in the bottle.

If milk is left to stand after milking, the fat rises to the top. The top part of the milk, rich in fat, is removed. It is called cream. Whipping cream from the store has from 32 percent to 40 percent fat. When air is whipped into it, whipping cream becomes thick enough to hold its shape.

The milk left when all the fat is removed is called skim milk. The fat content of whole milk, which still has cream in it, is adjusted so that it has 3.5 percent fat. Milk from the cow has from 3.6 percent to 6.1 percent fat. The whole milk is shaken up by special machines to break up the fat particles so the fat won't separate. This process is called homogenization. Milk sold in the store is also pasteurized—heated quickly to kill germs.

A stick of butter.

Many dairy products are made from milk. Butter is made by "churning" (beating or shaking) cream. Churning makes the fat separate from the liquid into lumps. The lumps are butter. They are collected and drained. Salt is usually added to the butter we eat before it is shaped into blocks for sale. The liquid left after the butter is removed is called buttermilk.

Cheese comes in more varieties than all other dairy products. There are hundreds of different kinds of cheeses in the world. To make cheese, rennet, a special material from calves' stomachs, is added to milk. The rennet makes the milk separate into a liquid part, the whey, and a solid part, the curds. The curds are collected and drained. They are treated differently to make many kinds of cheeses.

The solids from the milk are shaped into wheels, blocks, or balls while still wet and not completely set. These cheeses are then placed in a cool place for weeks or months. The longer the cheeses are left, or aged, the stronger they will taste.

The curds for making cheese are salted.

The wheels of cheese are aged in a cool place to develop flavor.

Some kinds, like bleu cheese, have special molds added to give them flavor. The mold grows slowly, changing the taste of the cheese. The blocks of other cheeses are soaked in flavorful mixtures of wine and herbs.

Yogurt is also made from milk. To make yogurt, milk is heated. Then a particular kind of bacteria is added. The mixture is kept warm for a few hours. The bacteria multiply, using the milk as food. As they grow, they change the milk's taste and thicken it. Sometimes, gelatin is added to make the yogurt firmer.

You can make yogurt at home. First the milk is heated to 115 degrees F.

Next, unpasteurized yogurt or dried starter is added to the milk.

The mixture is then placed in cups in a yogurt maker, which keeps it at the right temperature. When the yogurt is set, the cups are refrigerated.

CHAPTER SIX

Putting It All Together

Sometimes we eat food plain. For dinner we may have a piece of chicken, rice, some green peas, and a glass of milk. But mixing foods can be fun, too, and many favorite foods are combinations of different ingredients. A carrot cake, for example, contains carrots, a vegetable, and flour, from wheat grain. Eggs and milk from the dairy make it moist. The cake also has some fat, which could be vegetable oil or butter.

Combinations of foods result in many delicious things to eat, like these.

Sean likes yummy foods such as tacos.

Many of our tastiest foods are mixtures. Pizza dough is made from wheat, while the tomato sauce comes from a fruit. The sausage or pepperoni in the topping is mostly meat, while the cheese is from the dairy.

Tacos also have many different ingredients—tortillas from grain, chicken or beef filling, taco sauce from tomatoes and vegetables, and lettuce inside, all topped by tasty shredded cheese.

The next time you eat, why not try figuring out where your food comes from?

Index

(Numbers in *italics* refer to pages with illustrations.)